DISCIPLESHIP

—— IN ——

COACHING

Creating
Team Culture that
Builds Christian Character

DISCIPLESHIP
— IN —
COACHING

Dan Ellis

Cover designed by Dan Ellis and Danelle Young
Edited and formatted by Danelle Young, danelleyoung.com
Proofread by Staci Mauney, prestigeprose.com
Author portrait by Lifetouch

Discipleship in Coaching / Dan Ellis
ISBN: 979-8-9893880-0-4 (paperback)
ISBN: 979-8-9893880-1-1 (eBook)
Library of Congress Control Number: 2024904188

DEDICATION

To all the players I coached at Wood County Christian School.

To the administrative team I worked closely with at Wood County Christian School for many years:

    Robert L. Smith – Principal

    Jane Smith – Operations Administrator

    Mike Conaway – Athletic Director

    Kathy Carr – Financial Secretary

    Joy Smith – Athletic Secretary

To my wife, LaTrelle, who has lovingly supported me and our family.

To my daughter and editor, Danelle Young, who encouraged me to write this book.

To my son, Wade Ellis, whom I had the pleasure of coaching for four years at Wood County Christian School.

To Dan Morris, my faithful assistant, who coached for over twenty years in our basketball program at Wood County Christian School.

To Chuck Postlewait, a close brother in Christ who was a strong supporter of Wood County Christian School.

To Cam Hayes, a close Christian friend who sharpened my faith in the Lord.

To all the Christian coaches who will read this book and have a desire to be a positive influence for Christ in the lives of their players.

A good coach improves your game.
A great coach improves your life.

Michael Josephson

Contents

Chapter 1   PIONEERING........................1

Chapter 2   PRAYER 13

Chapter 3   PHILOSOPHY.................... 25

Chapter 4   PRINCIPLES 39

Chapter 5   PROVERBS......................... 53

Chapter 6   PRESENT............................ 71

Chapter 7   PLAYERS............................. 81

Chapter 8   PARENTS............................ 89

Chapter 9   PRACTICE.......................... 97

Chapter 10   PROMOTION 107

Chapter 1

PIONEERING

"Delight thyself also in the Lord: and he shall give thee the desires of thine heart." (Psalm 37:4)

When I look back on the twenty-two years I spent coaching varsity boys basketball at Wood County Christian School, I'm very grateful. God gave me the desires of my heart.

After I accepted Jesus Christ through faith as my personal Savior in my early twenties, the Lord opened doors for me to work with teenagers. I taught teen Sunday school classes, helped organize and supervise teen activities, served as a teen church camp counselor, and visited teens in their homes to encourage them in their faith.

DISCIPLESHIP IN COACHING

I remember one year I coached a group of teenage boys from our church in basketball. They enjoyed playing, but for one reason or another, they weren't on their high school basketball team. We met together, got organized, practiced, and I entered them into a high school basketball league at the YMCA. What a wonderful experience! I'd pick them up if they needed transportation, and that winter they played on a team. They enjoyed the game of basketball and Christian fellowship with each other. And it was a blessing to me to be a positive influence in their lives.

I had a desire to coach high school basketball and be a Christian influence, but because of my occupation, I assumed it wouldn't happen. I had a great job with a corporation in their marketing services department, which I enjoyed very much. I'd graduated from college with a Bachelor of Science in business administration and a double major in marketing and management. This job was perfect in relation to what I had studied. I was hired right out of college as a marketing trainee and was promoted several times to a position I enjoyed, working directly with our customers.

Like any job, the longer you do it, the more confident you become. I was very confident in my work, and my job was rewarding in many ways. I developed strong personal relationships with my customer contacts by applying the biblical principles of being honest and trustworthy. The Lord blessed my work. I was able to help my company and the companies we served be successful. I often thanked the Lord for my occupation and the job He gave me to support my family.

In 1995, the Lord brought together a group of pastors, parents, and educators in our area to begin a new Christian school. It was organized as a kindergarten through twelfth grade school and enrolled 175 students in the first year of operation. The name of the school was Wood County Christian School, and it was established in Williamstown, West Virginia, where a two-story building and eight acres of property were available.

We enrolled one of our two children in the school that first year and found out there was a need for a varsity boys basketball coach. The school had enough high school boys to start varsity basketball and soccer teams.

Ironically, I had worked with some of these boys on their basketball skills previously, knowing them through friendships at church. Because of that, the administration approached me about applying for the coaching position to help pioneer this new program. To make a long story short, I applied, received the job, and for the next twenty-two years had the privilege of being the varsity boys basketball coach at Wood County Christian School.

Starting out, we had no basketballs, no uniforms, and no gymnasium, but God provided everything we needed. God blessed us with a great group of young men that first year, willing to work hard and come together as a team. We finished that first season with a 20-6 record and finished runner-up in the West Virginia Christian Athletic Association Class A State Tournament. That team laid a solid foundation for our new program because the next season, we won the school's first state championship. "To God be the glory, great things He hath done!"[1]

First Varsity Boys Basketball Team

Front row left to right: Michael Cunningham, Jared Johnson, Josh Postlewait, Derrick Kapple, Paul Owens. Back row left to right: Coach Dan Ellis, Andy Wooddell, Jason Vannoy, John Smith, Jeff Morris, Travis Smith.

A sports reporter for a local newspaper wrote an article about our team entitled "The Road Warriors" because we had no gym at our school.

1. Fanny Crosby, "To God Be the Glory," (1875).

We had to rent gyms in the area for practice and home games. We played our home games in different gyms that we seldom got to practice in, but God blessed us and always provided for our needs. We operated like this for four more seasons before we finally built our own gymnasium on school property.

In my fourth season of coaching, I faced a career crossroads in my life. Another company had purchased the company I was working for and was eliminating our marketing services department in our area. They had their own marketing department in another state and asked me if I would move and relocate my family to work there.

By that time, Wood County Christian School had grown to the point where they were creating a new business administrator position. Because of that the administration approached me again about applying for this new position. My college background and business experience qualified me for the job. I would be a part of an administrative staff that loved the Lord and was pioneering new kingdom work through Christian education.

Chapter 1 - PIONEERING

There was still much to do to develop the school and campus.

Robert Smith, principal, and Jane Smith, operations administrator, were key administrative leaders in the pioneering of Wood County Christian School.

The school had just broken ground on a new high school building that included new classrooms, offices, a spacious gymnasium, a stage, locker rooms, and a handicapped-accessible elevator. The plan called for several phases of construction. A new cafeteria and more classrooms would be added when funds became available in the future.

Groundbreaking ceremony of new high school and gymnasium building

Artistic drawing of the planned new high school and gymnasium building

Chapter 1 - PIONEERING

After much prayer, Christian counsel, and discussions with my wife, LaTrelle, I decided to accept this new position at the school. I was seeking God's will for my life and my family and felt all these circumstances were leading me to serve the Lord in a full-time way. I believed the opportunity to serve at Wood County Christian School would contribute more to the Lord's work than the career path I was on.

LaTrelle and Dan Ellis

I remember finishing my corporate job on a Friday and starting my new job at the school on the following Monday. Soon after, our administration started a capital campaign and held the first annual Share the Vision Banquet to raise funds for the expansion of the school. Fundraising was critical in the development of our campus and academic programs. We were also able to secure several grants to help finance expansion. Because of God's provision through the years, the campus now accommodates over three hundred students and is fully accredited academically. We were also able to build that new cafeteria with additional classrooms onto the new high school and gymnasium building!

Completed new high school and gymnasium building

God not only allowed me the opportunity to pioneer a new basketball program but to contribute to the pioneering of a new Christian school. We serve a gracious and sovereign God.

First State Championship Team

Kneeling left to right: Brad Heidorn, Jeremy Fullerton, Paul Owens, Tim Fullerton, Michael Cunningham, Jared Johnson. Standing left to right: Coach Dan Ellis, Mitch Davis, Josh Postlewait, Josh Conaway, Jason Vannoy, Travis Smith, Duane Maze, Asst. Coach Don Heidorn.

WOOD COUNTY
CHRISTIAN SCHOOL
∽∽◇∽∽
1997 STATE CHAMPIONS
20 - 3
THANKS COACH ELLIS !

Chapter 2

PRAYER

"Call unto me, and I will answer thee, and show thee great and mighty things, which thou knowest not." (Jeremiah 33:3)

What a wonderful verse in Scripture that instructs us as Christians to talk directly to our heavenly Father in prayer!

We see in Jeremiah 33:3 that God was reminding Jeremiah, one of His prophets, to pray when Jeremiah was going through a difficult time in his life and ministry. King Zedekiah put him into prison for preaching the truth. The king and the people of Judah had drifted away from God and didn't want to hear the Word of God.

The first thing we see in this verse is a **prompting to pray**. Jeremiah is known as the weeping prophet because his heart was broken over the idolatry of the people of Judah. God prodded Jeremiah, "Call unto me." When Jeremiah was discouraged, disappointed, and disgraced, God reminded him to call on the Lord his Maker. Jeremiah knew to pray, and he did, but Jeremiah's discouraging circumstances were suppressing his prayer life.

The second thing we observe in this verse is the **promise of prayer**. God assured Jeremiah, "and I will answer thee." God answers the prayers of his children! Sometimes it's a direct answer. He promptly or precisely responds to our prayer request. We see an example of this in Elijah's prayer in I Kings 17:21–22 when he "cried unto the Lord, and said, O Lord my God, I pray thee, let this child's soul come into him again. And the Lord heard the voice of Elijah; and the soul of the child came into him again, and he revived." Sometimes it's a delayed answer. God answers our precise prayer request, but not immediately. In Daniel 10:10–15, God sent an angelic messenger to answer Daniel's prayer request, but the messenger had been delayed somewhere for twenty-one days before arriving. Daniel prayed for three weeks before receiving God's answer. Sometimes it's a denied answer. God doesn't answer our prayer because we ask amiss—meaning our motives are wrong or it isn't God's will. "Ye ask, and receive not, because ye ask amiss, that ye may consume it upon your lusts" (James 4:3). This is apparent in a prayer by the apostle Paul in 2 Corinthians 12:7–9. Paul prayed to the Lord three times to remove his "thorn in the flesh," but God gave him grace to endure it instead. He denied Paul's prayer request.

The third thing we notice in Jeremiah 33:3 is the **power of prayer**. God said, "I will show thee great and mighty things which thou knowest not." God is all-powerful, and He "is able to do exceeding abundantly above all we ask or think" (Ephesians 3:20). Jeremiah knew this! He had prayed previously to the Lord, saying, "Ah Lord God! Behold, thou hast made the heaven and the earth by thy great power and stretched out arm, and there is nothing too hard for thee" (Jeremiah 32:17). But at this moment, Jeremiah needed to be reminded that prayer activates God's power.

If God needed to prompt one of His prophets to pray, we certainly need prompting as well. Through the Word of God and His church, the Holy Spirit prompts us to pray, which is essential for our daily relationship with God.

Coaches, we have a great opportunity to lead by example and prompt our players to pray. To make prayer a priority for our teams. To incorporate prayer into our team meetings, practices, games, travels, tournaments, banquets, and one-on-one time with our players.

Begin by making a copy of your team roster and coaching staff so you can refer to it in your daily personal time of prayer. God gives a coach many hours to spend with his players, so it's likely a coach will learn of needs. Pray for those needs and ask God to perhaps use you to meet those needs.

I always kept close track of how my players were doing academically. I wanted them to maintain their eligibility and succeed in the classroom as well as on the court. Sometimes I had to meet individually with players to encourage them in their classes, and prayer was a part of those meetings. "Ye have not, because ye ask not" (James 4:2). "I can do all things through Christ which strengtheneth me" (Philippians 4:13). That begins with praying to our Heavenly Father in the name of Jesus, our Savior. I wanted to get across to our players that God could give them wisdom if they did their part in studying. "If any of you lack wisdom, let him ask of God, that giveth to all men liberally" (James 1:5). The God who knows all things can help our players learn and be successful in the classroom.

We strived to make prayer a daily part of our practice. We would begin and end with prayer. We also prayed before games and after games. Prayer helped prepare us for the task at hand. Prayer helped us stay focused on our goal of glorifying God in all that we did. We wanted to glorify God in the way we practiced and played our games. We wanted to develop a culture of keeping God in the forefront of our minds, and prayer helped us do that.

Prayer also brought our teams closer together. We would set aside time just for prayer. If any of our players had individual needs, we would pray for those needs. If any of our players were injured, we would pray for God's healing. If any of our players had family concerns, we would pray for those concerns. If any of our players had issues among themselves, we wanted to resolve them through counsel and prayer. "Confess your faults one to

Players praying prior to a home game

Chapter 2 - PRAYER

One of our players leading in prayer at our sports banquet

another, and pray one for another, that ye may be healed" (James 5:16). A family that prays together stays together. Our goal was to be a family.

I remember one year our senior point guard seriously injured his knee in a game with a month remaining in our schedule. He was one of our key players, and we were concerned his high school career was over. However, through much prayer, a month of rest, and a bulky brace, he was able to come back for our postseason and help our team win the West Virginia Christian Class AA State

Tournament. Not only did he play, he made the All-Tournament team because of how well he played. A few days later, our team played and won the NACA Division II National Tournament in Dayton, Tennessee. Again, he made the All-Tournament team. It was incredible witnessing that amazing answer to our prayers! He wasn't without pain, but he was able to play through his injury and finish the season, which is what we prayed for. We serve and worship an all-powerful God who hears and answers our prayers according to his will.

Through the years I was at Wood County Christian School, I saw the Lord do great and mighty things through prayer! I attribute the success of our basketball program to answered prayer. I believe our fundraising success and the development of our campus are answers to prayer. I believe the success of our school's accredited academic program is a result of prayer. "Every good gift and every perfect gift is from above, and cometh down from the Father" (James 1:17). "The effectual fervent prayer of a righteous man availeth much" (James 5:16). "Let us therefore come boldly unto the throne of grace, that we may obtain mercy, and find grace to help in time of need" (Hebrews 4:16).

In Recognition of Our 1998 State Championship and NACA National Championship Team

Sitting left to right: Paul Owens, David Brooks, Wade Ellis, Michael Cunningham. Kneeling left to right: Elijah Colgrove, Josh Garrett, Ryan Harnish, Brad Heidorn. Standing left to right: Asst. Coach Mike Conaway, Duane Maze, Jared Johnson, Josh Conaway, Travis Smith, Tim Fullerton, Head Coach Dan Ellis.

DISCIPLESHIP IN COACHING

*Left to right: Senior tri-captains Jared Johnson,
Paul Owens, and Travis Smith*

DISCIPLESHIP IN COACHING

The team was invited to the West Virginia State Capital and recognized by Governor Cecil Underwood after winning the NACA National Championship.

Left to right: Coach Dan Ellis, senior Duane Maze, and senior Michael Cunningham

Chapter 3

PHILOSOPHY

"According to the grace of God which is given unto me, as a wise masterbuilder, I have laid the foundation, and another buildeth thereon. But let every man take heed how he buildeth thereupon. For other foundation can no man lay than that is laid, which is Jesus Christ." (1 Cor. 3:10–11)

A solid foundation is important when building anything, and it starts with a blueprint. When I began thinking about pioneering a new basketball program, I felt like I needed to spell out my philosophy of coaching basketball. This was my blueprint for building the program's foundation. I did this before I even applied for the new coaching position at Wood County Christian School. When I did apply, I included a copy of my philosophy with my application.

My philosophy included seven main points that helped me stay focused on what we were trying to accomplish with each team. I followed the blueprint each season.

The first and most important point of my philosophy was to **emphasize being a good testimony for Christ**. We know from reading earlier in I Corinthians 3:11 that "other foundation can no man lay than that is laid, which is Jesus Christ." I wanted players to understand the foundation of our team was Jesus and how important being a good testimony for Christ was. I knew it had to begin with me. And I expected our players to strive to be a good testimony as well. First Corinthians 10:31 says, "Whatsoever ye do, do all to the glory of God." This is done in sports by coaches emphasizing good sportsmanship, self-control, a diligent effort, and Christ-like character, including patience, perseverance, obedience, excellence, humbleness, and faithfulness. These were things we would talk about and emphasize throughout the season.

The remaining six points in my coaching philosophy were geared toward coaching basketball but can apply to coaching any sport. The way we carried out these next six points correlated with how successful each team was. Coaching was always fun for me because I enjoyed the process. I enjoyed the journey of each season. These next six points were keys to the process of molding and developing teams. They're not profound, but they're essential for success. Our goal was for each team to become their very best with the God-given talent they had, and every team was different.

With that said, the second point of my philosophy was to **emphasize the fundamentals of basketball.** There's an expression: "You must learn to walk before you can run!" In any sport, you must learn the fundamentals to excel at playing the game. NBA star Larry Bird said, "First master the fundamentals!" Michael Jordan, another NBA great, said, "Get the fundamentals down, and the level of everything you do will rise." In basketball, the fundamentals of shooting, dribbling, passing, catching, rebounding, screening, and defending are vitally important to the success of teams. We would spend at least half of our practices using different drills to teach and improve those fundamentals. The sooner players learn *proper* fundamentals, the more skilled they'll become as they grow and mature. Our goal every season was to be sound fundamentally. When you have a group of players that are skilled in the fundamentals of any sport, your chances of success increase.

The third point was to **emphasize and develop physical conditioning**. Your players must be in excellent physical condition to excel as a team. Jogging, stretching, running, weightlifting, proper rest, proper diet, and maintaining good health are key. Our goal was to get our players into basketball shape and to be ready to compete. We would start practices with some light warm-up drills for about ten minutes to get our players' muscles warmed up and then go into stretching exercises. Routine stretching helps increase your flexibility and betters overall movement. It also helps prevent injuries as players progress into a more intense practice. Gradually prepare a team for a physical workout or practice. Once our players had warmed up, we would pick up the pace. You've heard the expression, "The way you practice is the way you play the game." Our goal was to gradually rev up our practices to game-like speed. Drills and speed intensified until we felt our players had a good physical workout. Once our game schedule started, we were also cautious about not overworking teams, especially the night before a game. The goal was always to prepare them to excel physically at game time!

The fourth point was to **emphasize and develop mental preparation**. We taught offensive strategies like plays, proper spacing, and positioning to our players so they were mentally ready to execute. We wanted our players to be prepared to counter any type of defense we would face in a game. How to attack a man-to-man defense. How to attack a 2-3 zone defense. How to attack a 3-2 zone defense. How to attack a 1-3-1 zone defense. How to break different presses. What plays to run in out-of-bounds situations, under the basket, or on the side of the court. Our goal was to prepare our players mentally for any situation and what to do in the positions they were playing. On the flip side, we wanted to teach defensive strategies with man to man and zone coverage. Like in a successful offense, players carry out individual responsibilities when playing good defense. We worked daily in practice to develop mental confidence by teaching these offensive and defensive strategies and repeating them.

The fifth point was to **emphasize and develop teamwork**. To do this, a coach needs to clearly teach each player's position and responsibilities. Like a lot of teams, we used the numbering system to teach and identify each position: (1) point guard, (2) shooting guard, (3) small forward, (4) power forward, and (5) center. We used these numbers in our strategies for both offense and defense to clearly teach what each player's responsibility was. We first had to identify what position or positions each player was best suited for and then clearly teach that position's role for the team. All the positions complement one another, and a coach needs to constantly encourage an unselfish spirit to develop teamwork. A basketball team is like the five fingers on your hand. They're all different, but when they come together into a grip, they work together in a powerful way! That's what teamwork is all about—coming together to work powerfully.

The sixth point was to **emphasize and develop a fun environment**. Basketball, like many sports, is a fun game to play for enjoyment, exercise, and camaraderie. We wanted our players to have a fun experience! We always included some shooting drills in practice—dividing up into teams to have some fun competition. Players would shoot at different spots on the floor to see which team made twenty shots first. The losers had to run laps! We would have similar competitions to practice free throws. We also had some individual competitions like a fun game of Knockout that helps develop quick shooting skills under pressure. Occasionally, we had a 3-on-3 tournament, which our players always enjoyed, and of course, 5-on-5 scrimmages.

We used a multitude of drills and knew which drills our players enjoyed the most.

We also liked to spice up our schedule each year to make it fun. Twice we went to play a game at Quicken Loans Arena (presently known as Rocket Mortgage FieldHouse) in Cleveland, Ohio before a Cleveland Cavaliers game and then stayed to watch the Cavaliers and LeBron James play. Our players, students, parents, and fans loved this experience.

Wood County Christian Night with the Cavaliers!

Come to Quicken Loans Arena on February 27th and cheer on the Wood County Christian boys and girls basketball teams as they play Licking County Christian on the Cavaliers court! With this special offer, you can save up to $8 on each ticket!

Following the Wood County Christian game, we invite you to sit back and enjoy as the Cavaliers take on the New Orleans/Oklahoma Hornets!

Wood County Christian vs. LCCA
Tip off at 2:15PM

Cavaliers vs. Hornets
Tuesday, February 27th, 2007
7:00 PM Tip Off

Two Packages to Choose From:

Price	Includes:	Price	Includes:
$27	Admittance to the WCCS game $35 Upper Side ticket for Cavaliers game	**$20**	Admittance to the WCCS game $25 Upper Corner ticket for Cavaliers game

Due to limited inventory, orders **MUST** be received by January 29th
This game will be a SELL OUT! Don't delay, order today!

To order, please contact the Wood County Christian School Athletic Office or WCCS Varsity Boys or Girls Players
Please make checks out to Wood County Christian School
Orders **MUST** be received by: January 29th, 2007

We went to several Christian universities and colleges through the years to play in their eight-team tournaments, which was always fun. It was also an opportunity for our players to stay and visit each Christian campus. On one occasion, we held a fundraiser to fly our team from Pittsburgh International Airport to Pensacola Christian College in Pensacola, Florida, to play in their tournament. That was fun because it was a first-time flying experience for most of our team.

We tried to include various tournaments in our schedule each season. Some of those tournaments were local, but the majority were overnight trips, which were fun for our players and built camaraderie. Through the years, we competed in different tournaments in West Virginia, Ohio, Michigan, Pennsylvania, Virginia, Tennessee, South Carolina, and Florida.

Almost every year I coached, we played in the West Virginia Hoops Classic, which was usually held at the Charleston Civic Center, one of the largest arenas in the state. This was an exciting opportunity for our players. For many of those

Hoops Classic games, we provided transportation for our team and the students who went to support us. It was a fun experience for everyone.

According to a 2014 George Washington University study, nine out of ten kids listed "having fun" as their number one priority in sports.[2] Coaches should try to create an encouraging and positive atmosphere to make this happen.

The seventh and final point was to **be organized for practice**. We wanted to make the most of the practice time allotted to us on the court. You've heard the expression, "Manage your time, or your time will manage you." It's important as coaches to do our best to manage the time we have for practice. I drafted a basketball practice schedule prior to practice that included everything we wanted to accomplish and do that day. I allotted time to each task, and we used our scoreboard clock to keep us on schedule. We limited most of our drills to five minutes and varied them to develop different skills. We tried to stress how important it was to be

2. "Why Kids Quit Sports," Changing the Game Project, May 5, 2015, https://changingthegameproject.com/why-kids-quit-sports/.

dressed and on time for practice, and we made it a point to finish on time. Punctuality is important in life. Coaches have a great opportunity to teach this and hold their players accountable.

In Recognition of Our 2000 State Championship Team

Kneeling left to right holding banner: Asst. Coach Mike Conaway, Head Coach Dan Ellis. Standing left to right: Tony Postlewait, Jared Morris, Ryan Harnish, Josh Garrett, Josh Conaway, Davey Fore, Brad Heidorn, Joey Johnston, Wade Ellis, Andrew Schulze.

*Robert Smith, principal, taking his turn
cutting down the net*

Coach Dan Ellis

Left to right: Athletic Director/Asst. Coach Mike Conaway, Head Coach Dan Ellis, Asst. Coach Don Heidorn

Presentation of state championship plaque, banner, and game ball

PHILOSOPHY OF COACHING BASKETBALL

by Dan Ellis

I. Emphasize Being a Good Testimony for Christ

    A. "Whatever ye do, do all to the glory of God." I Corinthians 10:31

        1. Good sportsmanship

        2. Self-control

        3. Diligent effort

        4. Christ-like character

          a. patient, persevering, obedient, faithful, humble, excellence

II. Emphasize the Fundamentals of Basketball

    A. Shooting, dribbling, passing, catching, rebounding, screening.

    B. Use different drills to teach and improve these fundamentals.

    C. Work on these fundamentals regularly in practice.

III. Emphasize and Develop Physical Conditioning

    A. Stretching

    B. Running

    C. Weights

    D. Proper rest and diet

IV. Emphasize and Develop Mental Preparation

    A. Teaching offensive strategies with plays and positioning

    B. Teaching defensive strategies with man to man and zone coverage

    C. Develop mental confidence by repetition and practice.

V. Emphasize and Develop Teamwork

    A. Clearly teach each player's position and responsibilities.

    B. Clearly explain each player's role on the team.

    C. Encourage an unselfish spirit within the team.

VI. Emphasize and Develop a Fun Environment

    A. Basketball is a fun game for enjoyment, exercise, and camaraderie.

VII. Be Organized for Practice

    A. To accomplish team goals and get the most out of time invested.

DiscipleshipInCoaching.com

Chapter 4

PRINCIPLES

"Therefore leaving the principles of the doctrine of Christ, let us go on unto perfection." (Hebrews 6:1)

As Christians, God wants us to progress toward spiritual maturity applying the principles taught in His Word. The Bible is full of Christian values, which are principles we strive to live by daily. These Christian values help shape and develop our character. They are opposed by worldly values. For example, Jesus taught forgiveness rather than revenge, love in lieu of hate, honesty instead of dishonesty, and diligence over laziness. These and other Christian values are taught in the Bible.

DISCIPLESHIP IN COACHING

What a great opportunity we have as Christian coaches to relay and reinforce Christian values to our players! We can help build their character using the doctrines of Christ, and that could be life-changing for kids. Michael Josephson, President of the CHARACTER COUNTS! Coalition said, "A good coach improves your game. A great coach improves your life." We have chances to improve lives by reinforcing Christian values.

Several years ago, I did a study on Christian values taught in the Bible and came up with close to seventy. I arranged them in alphabetical order and had at least one Bible verse for each value. For example, I came up with several words that begin with D: *dependability* (Daniel 6:4), *desire* (Psalm 37:4), *determination* (2 Chronicles 2:1), *devotion* (Psalm 119:38), *diligence* (Proverbs 12:24), and *discipline* (I Corinthians 9:27). I ended up with Christian values for almost every letter of the alphabet. God wants us to apply these toward spiritual maturity.

My coaching staff and I periodically shared some of these Christian values in practice with

Chapter 4 - PRINCIPLES

CHRISTIAN VALUES

Christian values are principles that followers of Christ strive to live by daily.

Accountability	(Proverbs 27:17)	Industrious	(Proverbs 6:6-8)
Alertness	(II Timothy 4:5)	Initiative	(James 4:17)
Attentiveness	(Proverbs 4:20)	Integrity	(Proverbs 19:1)
Adaptability	(I Corinthians 9:20-23)	Joyful	(Proverbs 17:22)
Commitment	(I Peter 2:21-24)	Kindness	(Romans 12:10)
Compassion	(Luke 10:33)	Loyalty	(Proverbs 17:17)
Confidence	(Proverbs 3:26)	Love	(I Corinthians 13)
Consistency	(I Corinthians 15:58)	Merciful	(Psalm 25:10)
Cooperation	(Philemon 24)	Meekness	(Titus 3:2)
Courage	(II Samuel 10:12)	Obedient	(Hebrews 13:17)
Courteous	(I Peter 3:8)	Orderly	(I Corinthians 14:40)
Dependability	(Daniel 6:4)	Patience	(Hebrews 12:1)
Desire	(Psalm 37:4)	Perseverance	(Ephesians 6:18)
Determination	(II Chronicles 2:1)	Persistence	(Luke 11:9-10)
Devotion	(Psalm 119:38)	Poise	(Philippians 4:6-7)
Diligent	(Proverbs 12:24)	Positive	(Philippians 4:13)
Discerning	(Hebrews 5:14)	Prayerful	(James 5:16)
Discipline	(Job 35:10)	Prepared	(I Peter 3:15)
Enthusiasm	(Colossians 3:23)	Prompt	(Ecclesiastes 9:1)
Excellence	(Daniel 6:3)	Reliability	(Luke 16:19)
Encouraging	(Hebrews 10:24-25)	Respectful	(Malachi 1:6)
Fairness	(I Timothy 5:21)	Responsible	(Nehemiah 7:2)
Faithful	(I Corinthians 4:2)	Self-Control	(Proverbs 25:28)
Friendly	(Proverbs 8:24)	Selfless	(Philemon 2:4)
Forgiving	(Ephesians 4:32)	Submissive	(James 4:7)
Fearless	(Isaiah 41:10)	Teachable	(Proverbs 10:14)
Flexibility	(Genesis 12:1)	Tenderhearted	(Ephesians 4:32)
Fortitude	(Proverbs 28:1)	Thankful	(I Thessalonians 5:18)
Giving	(Luke 6:38)	Trustworthy	(Psalm 118:8)
God-fearing	(Proverbs 9:10)	Unity	(Psalm 133:1)
Honesty	(Proverbs 12:22)	Unselfish	(Philippians 2:4)
Honor	(I Peter 2:17)	Virtuous	(II Peter 1:5)
Humility	(Proverbs 22:4)	Zealous	(Colossians 3:23)

DiscipleshipInCoaching.com

our players but later chose five to become our core values. Those five core values were the core of our culture. Our goal was to build our teams around those five core values. We gave a copy of the five values to each player and went over them before the season. I posted them on the walls of our locker room as reminders. We reinforced those core values when we could. Those core values helped us define the type of team we wanted to become and how to be a good testimony for Christ. Former Duke University head coach Mike Krzyzewski said, "Don't take culture for granted. There needs to be a constant renewal of values that leads to camaraderie." Those five core values were a constant renewal of who we wanted to be together as a team.

Our first core value was **honor**. Honor means showing respect for others. We would tell our players that, above all, we wanted to honor God. That should be our goal as individuals and as a team. But beyond that, they should honor their parents, teachers, teammates, classmates, coaches, game officials, and opponents. We didn't condone trash talk from our players to our opponents. Let your game do the talking! We are to "Honour all men" (I Peter 2:17), and that includes the opposing team. I always tried to show respect to my opposing coach and make him feel welcome. I would make it a point to greet and talk to opposing coaches before and after games. I also wanted to show respect to officials refereeing our games. I was once an official myself, and officials are trying their best to enforce the rules of the game, like we're trying our best to coach our teams. None of us are perfect. There's a way to communicate with officials without being disrespectful if a coach doesn't agree with a call.

Our second core value was **diligence**. Diligence means working hard to accomplish a task. In our case, it was working hard to become the best team we could be for the glory of God. Proverbs 12:24 teaches that "the hand of the diligent shall bear rule." That's teaching a principle—if you work hard in life, the results will probably pay off in a positive way. The difference between ordinary and extraordinary is that little extra! We wanted our teams to work hard in practice so they would be successful in games. We constantly reminded our players of their next opponent. Were they working harder in practice to prepare for us than we were working to prepare for them? Your toughest competitor in life is anyone who will work harder than you. Benjamin Franklin said, "Diligence overcomes difficulties; sloth make them." God honors hard work and encourages it in his Word. "For thou shalt eat the labour of thine hands: happy shalt thou be, and it shall be well with thee" (Psalm 128:2).

Our third core value was **faithfulness**. Faithful means to be dependable and trustworthy. I encouraged our players to be faithful to God, family, friends, teammates, and coaches. First Corinthians 4:2 says, "Moreover it is required in stewards, that a man be found faithful." A coach must set the example for his team by being faithful to them. Being a person they can trust and depend on. We wanted our players to be faithful to one another and our coaching staff. Like any team, if players aren't faithful to be at practice or maintain their eligibility, it's going to hurt the whole team. A chain is only as strong as the weakest link. The weakest link on your team affects the performance of the whole team. Teamwork depends on good timing and synchronization. The plays we run take hours of practice to learn, become effective, and maintain. If one key player isn't faithful to be at practice, it affects the other players and coaches who are. The best ability is dependability, and that's true in life as well as sports.

Our fourth core value was **unselfishness**. Unselfish is putting others ahead of yourself. Philippians 2:3 says, "In lowliness of mind let each esteem others better than themselves." The core value of being unselfish is what molds a group of players into a team. It's a team-before-me attitude that elevates everyone. Below is a TEAM acrostic that says it well.

Together

Everyone

Achieves

More

John Wooden, former UCLA head basketball coach who won ten national championships, said, "The main ingredient of stardom is the rest of the team." Teamwork is what elevates an individual player to the next level. Former Boston Celtics Head Coach Red Auerbach said, "Some say you have to use your five best players, but I found out you win with the five that fit together best as a team." The most successful teams I coached at Wood County Christian School were the teams that were the most unselfish. They didn't care who scored, as long as we scored. Players passed up good shots for better shots. The five on the floor moved the ball until they found an open man. In most cases, teams that play unselfishly will have three or four players average in double figures by the end of the season. A rising tide lifts all boats! Teamwork lifts all players! Teamwork is what makes a team work! It all starts with the Christian value of being unselfish.

Our fifth core value was **perseverance**. Perseverance is not quitting during difficult circumstances. First Corinthians 15:58 says, "Be ye steadfast, unmovable, always abounding in the work of the Lord." That verse is teaching perseverance. A true competitor never quits; he keeps competing. Well-known author and speaker John C. Maxwell said, "The only guarantee for failure is to stop trying." Inventor Thomas Edison said,

Chapter 4 - PRINCIPLES

**The Core Values of
Wood County Christian School
Boys Basketball**

Core Values	Definition	Scripture	Quote
Honor	Demonstrating respect to others (To God, parents, teachers, teammates, classmates, coaches, opponents, and referees)	"Honor all men." (I Peter 2:17)	"Treat others as you want to be treated." (Lou Holtz, former coach)
Diligence	Working hard to accomplish a task (To become the best team God desires us to be)	"The hand of the diligent shall bear rule." (Prov. 12:24)	"The difference between ordinary and extraordinary is that little extra!" (unknown)
Faithfulness	Being reliable, dependable, and trustworthy to others (To God, family, teammates, and coaches)	"Moreover it is required in stewards, that a man be found faithful." (1 Cor. 4:2)	"The best ability is dependability!" (unknown)
Unselfishness	Putting others ahead of yourself (A team before me attitude)	"In lowliness of mind let each esteem others better than themselves." (Phil. 2:3)	"The main ingredient of stardom is the rest of the team." (John Wooden, former coach)
Perseverance	Not quitting during difficult circumstances	"Be steadfast, unmoveable, always abounding in the work of the Lord." (1 Cor. 15:58)	A true competitor never quits; he keeps competing! (unknown)

Coach Dan Ellis

DiscipleshipInCoaching.com

"Many of life's failures are people who did not realize how close they were to success when they gave up." Helen Keller, a blind American author and lecturer, said, "A bend in the road is not the end of the road unless you fail to make the turn." A season and even one game can have a lot of ups and downs. Perseverance is a Christian value that helps a team press on. I always encouraged our teams to play hard to the very end.

We witnessed some unbelievable comeback victories because our team persevered and kept competing. We were in games where we were down double digits and came back to win. One such time was a game we played in Cleveland, Ohio, prior to a Cleveland Cavaliers game. We were down seventeen points with three minutes to go in the third quarter and came back to win the game! I witnessed some exciting comeback victories over the years, but that one might have been the most dramatic! After the game, a sportswriter interviewed one of our senior players who said, "We hustled. We knew we had to pick it up. We just didn't want to lose." That's perseverance! That's what we call mental toughness—not giving up during difficult circumstances. When you have a group of players with that kind of mindset, sometimes the impossible becomes possible.

Chapter 4 - PRINCIPLES

There are other Christian values taught in Scripture that Christian coaches can teach or use as core values for their team. The point is Christian values are principles we should strive to live by and promote to our players. We all want to build character and have successful teams. The principles of the doctrines of Christ help us do that.

In Recognition of Our 2001 State Championship and NACA National Final Four Team

Sitting left to right: Davey Fore, Wade Ellis, Jared Morris, Josh Garrett, Tony Postlewait. Standing left to right: Head Coach Dan Ellis, Asst. Coach Dan Morris, David Boney, Zach Gibson, John Rodgers, Patrick Perine, Andrew Schulze, Jim Ashley, Asst. Coach Mike Conaway, Asst. Coach Rick Smith.

Left to right: 2001 senior tri-captains Jared Morris,
Josh Garrett, Wade Ellis

Chapter 5

PROVERBS

"The proverbs ... To know wisdom and instruction ... to the young man knowledge and discretion." (Proverbs 1:1–4)

A biblical proverb is a sentence that gives practical advice based on divine revelation. A human proverb is a sentence that gives practical advice based on human experience.

Proverbs are always good to share with your team. They provide knowledge and help build character. Use one to help emphasize a point you want to get across. The goal is to share knowledge that young people can apply toward wisdom. I liked to share proverbs with our players, and they were always well received.

For example, I shared Proverbs 12:24 most years to encourage our players to be hard-working and to have a diligent mindset in practice and games. "The hand of the diligent shall bear rule." We wanted our players to have a good work ethic. One particular year, that verse seemed to register more than others because I overheard our players quoting and encouraging each other with it during the season.

Following is a collection of proverbs I like on leadership, teamwork, and character. Some may benefit you personally and others your players. Hopefully, you'll find some in this collection for both. Use this chapter as a reference when choosing a *Proverb/Thought for the Day* for your practice schedule (printable PDF included on page 116).

LEADERSHIP

"Iron sharpeneth iron; so a man sharpeneth the countenance of his friend." (Proverbs 27:17)

"I lead in the way of righteousness." (Proverbs 8:20)

"The integrity of the upright shall guide them." (Proverbs 11:3)

"When the righteous are in authority, the people rejoice: but when the wicked beareth rule, the people mourn." (Proverbs 29:2)

"He that walketh with wise men shall be wise: but a companion of fools shall be destroyed." (Proverbs 13:20)

"A friend loveth at all times, and a brother is born for adversity." (Proverbs 17:17)

"Everything rises and falls on leadership." (John C. Maxwell)

"As a leader, you can be demanding without being demeaning." (Don Meyer)

"Leadership is influence." (John C. Maxwell)

"A good leader takes a little more than his share of the blame, a little less than his share of the credit." (Arnold Glasnow)

"A leader is one who knows the way, goes the way, and shows the way." (John C. Maxwell)

"A leader's success is largely determined by the ability to motivate others." (Unknown)

"Good leadership isn't about advancing yourself. It's about advancing your team." (John C. Maxwell)

"Leaders look beyond themselves, focusing on the people they lead and where they should be going together." (Tony Dungy)

"Character is the foundation on which leadership is built." (Tony Dungy)

"Leaders keep the vision and mission out front." (Tony Dungy)

"Attitudes are contagious . . . Are yours worth catching?" (Dennis Mannering)

"Leadership is unlocking people's potential to become better." (Bill Bradley)

"Great leadership is about uniting a team, not dividing one." (Unknown)

"Earn your leadership every day." (Michael Jordan)

"Become the kind of person that people would follow voluntarily even if you had no title or position." (Brian Tracy)

"Do not deny the impact your life can have on others." (Dave Dravecky)

"I think one of the keys to leadership is recognizing that everyone has gifts and talents. A good leader will learn how to harvest those gifts toward the same goal." (Dr. Ben Carson)

"Remember that mentor leadership is all about serving. Jesus said, 'For even the Son of Man came not to be served but to serve others and to give his life as a ransom for many' (Mark 10:45)." (Tony Dungy)

"Engage, educate, equip, encourage, empower, energize, and elevate. Those are methods for maximizing the potential of any individual, team, organization, or institution for ultimate success and significance. Those are the methods of a mentor leader." (Tony Dungy)

TEAMWORK

"Where no counsel is, the people fall: but in the multitude of counsellors there is safety." (Proverbs 11:14)

"Two are better than one; because they have a good reward for their labour." (Ecclesiastes 4:9)

"A threefold cord is not quickly broken." (Ecclesiastes 4:12)

"Behold, how good and how pleasant it is for brethren to dwell together in unity!" (Psalm 133:1)

"But now are they many members, yet but one body." (I Corinthians 12:20)

"And let us consider one another to provoke unto love and to good works." (Hebrews 10:24)

"If everyone is moving forward together, then success takes care of itself." (Henry Ford)

"Alone we can do little, together we can do much." (Helen Keller)

"Talent wins games, but teamwork and intelligence win championships." (Michael Jordan)

"If you want to lift yourself up, lift up someone else." (Booker T. Washington)

"Coming together is the beginning. Keeping together is progress. Working together is success." (Henry Ford)

"The strength of the team is each individual member. The strength of each member is the team." (Phil Jackson)

"There is no 'I' in Team, but there is an 'E' for Everyone. A team achieves more when everyone contributes." (Robert Cheeke)

"This is a team game, and one man doesn't win and one man doesn't lose. In the end, the best team usually wins." (Wilt Chamberlain)

"Some say you have to use your five best players, but I found out you win with the five that fit together best as a team." (Red Auerbach)

"The main ingredient of stardom is the rest of the team." (John Wooden)

"Teamwork is the fuel that allows common people to produce uncommon results." (Unknown)

"Good teams become great ones when the members trust each other enough to surrender the 'me' for the 'we.'" (Phil Jackson)

"A single arrow is easily broken, but not ten in a bundle." (Japanese proverb)

"It is amazing what you can accomplish if no one cares who gets the credit." (Harry Truman)

"Teamwork makes the dream work." (John C. Maxwell)

"Teamwork makes the team work." (Unknown)

"Your team will reach its potential only if you reach your potential." (John C. Maxwell)

"If you think you're the entire picture, you will never see the big picture." (John C. Maxwell)

"You are most valuable where you add the most value." (John C. Maxwell)

"Winning teams have players who make things happen." (John C. Maxwell)

"Great teams have great teammates!" (Unknown)

CHARACTER

"Trust in the Lord with all thine heart" (Proverbs 3:5). *Be saved.*

"The fear of the Lord is the beginning of wisdom" (Proverbs 9:10). *Be God-fearing.*

"The hand of the diligent shall bear rule" (Proverbs 12:24). *Be hard-working.*

"Wise men lay up knowledge" (Proverbs 10:14). *Be teachable.*

"By humility and the fear of the Lord are riches, and honour, and life" (Proverbs 22:4). *Be humble.*

"The eyes of the Lord are in every place, beholding the evil and the good" (Proverbs 15:3). *Beware—God is watching.*

"A man that hath friends must show himself friendly" (Proverbs 18:24). *Be friendly.*

"Lying lips are abomination to the Lord" (Proverbs 12:22). *Be honest.*

"A faithful man shall abound with blessings" (Proverbs 28:20). *Be faithful.*

"The true expression of Christian character is not in good-doing but in Christ-likeness." (Oswald Chambers)

"What you are as a person is far more important than what you are as a basketball player." (John Wooden)

"The true test of a man's character is what he does when no one is watching." (John Wooden)

"Ability may get you to the top, but it takes character to keep you there." (John Wooden)

"Be more concerned with your character than your reputation, because your character is what you really are, while your reputation is merely what others think you are." (John Wooden)

"Discipline yourself, and others won't have to." (John Wooden)

"Nothing will work unless you do." (John Wooden)

"Failing to prepare is preparing to fail." (John Wooden)

"Talent is God-given. Be humble. Fame is man-given. Be grateful. Conceit is self-given. Be careful." (John Wooden)

"All of us learned to walk by failing." (J. R. Rim)

"The best motivation always comes from within." (Michael Johnson)

"There may be people that have more talent than you, but there's no excuse for anyone to work harder than you do." (Derek Jeter)

"Losers quit when they fail; winners fail until they succeed." (Robert Kiyosaki)

"Well done is better than well said." (Benjamin Franklin)

Chapter 5 - PROVERBS

"Present choices determine future consequences." (Unknown)

"Confidence is contagious." (Vince Lombardi)

"Rule your mind, or it will rule you." (Horace)

"Good attitudes among players do not guarantee a team's success, but bad attitudes guarantee its failure." (John C. Maxwell)

"True humility is not thinking less of yourself; it is thinking of yourself less." (C. S. Lewis)

"The difference between ordinary and extraordinary is that little extra." (Unknown)

"The best ability is dependability." (Unknown)

"A true competitor never quits; he keeps competing!" (Unknown)

"Hard work is not punishment. Hard work is the price of admission for the opportunity to reach sustained excellence." (Jay Bilas)

"The greatest compliment to any player is he is a great teammate. We can't all be great players, but we can all be great teammates." (Jay Bilas)

Left to right: La Trelle Ellis, Jay Bilas (former professional basketball player, coach, and current ESPN college basketball analyst), and Coach Dan Ellis

Chapter 5 - PROVERBS

In Recognition of Our 2004 State
Championship Team

Sitting front row left to right: Nathan Lord, Daniel Smith, Seth Wilson, Michael Johnson, Aaron Wilson, John Gainer. Back row standing left to right: Head Coach Dan Ellis, Todd Hughes, Asst. Coach Alan Carroll, Nathan Heiney, Kyle Bichard, John Mark Conaway, Andrew Ashley, Asst. Coach Dan Morris, Joseph Ward, Asst. Coach Mike Conaway.

DISCIPLESHIP IN COACHING

Chapter 6

PRESENT

"I beseech you therefore, brethren, by the mercies of God, that ye present your bodies a living sacrifice, holy, acceptable unto God, which is your reasonable service. And be not conformed to this world: but be ye transformed by the renewing of your mind, that ye may prove what is that good, and acceptable, and perfect, will of God."
(Romans 12:1-2)

Romans 12 is an excellent chapter in the Bible to instruct us toward discipleship in coaching. Discipleship is all about building relationships: our relationship with God and our relationships with others. Our relationship with God helps us build our relationship with others the right way and become effective disciples for Christ.

In Romans 12:1–3, we see our relationship with God. In Romans 12:4–21, we see our relationship with others. How we obey the first three verses affects how successful we'll be in living out the rest of the verses in this chapter.

Regarding our relationship with God, we see first in Romans 12:1 there needs to be a **daily devotion** to God. The apostle Paul is writing to Christians, addressing them as brethren. These brethren had been justified by faith in Jesus, as Paul alluded to earlier in Romans 5:1. His desire now was for these brethren to *present* (devote) themselves to live daily for the Lord. He used the word *beseech,* which means to exhort—to strongly urge someone to act. Considering God's mercy and gift of salvation, the least they could do was *present* (devote) their bodies to live sacrificially for Him. This was reasonable. "Discipline says, 'I need to.' Duty says, 'I ought to.' Devotion says, 'I want to'" (Adrian Rogers). We should "want to" *present* (devote) ourselves daily to live for our Lord and Savior Jesus Christ.

I remember hearing a preacher say when he woke up each day, before his feet hit the floor, he would thank the Lord for another day and pray, "I give my life for your service." That should be our attitude, at least, as we live each day. What a great mindset! God wants to use us for his service. Present (devote) yourself daily to live for the Lord. It should be our natural response to what he's done for us.

In verse 2, Paul takes it a step further and says there needs to be a **daily transformation**. He says don't be conformed to this world system that is anti-God. Be transformed daily by the renewing of your mind so you can do God's will. When we're born again, the Holy Spirit comes into our lives and begins to transform (change) us. "Know ye not that your body is the temple of the Holy Ghost which is in you, which ye have of God, and ye are not your own? For ye are bought with a price; therefore glorify God in your body, and in your spirit, which are God's" (I Corinthians 6:19–20).

God wants us to glorify Him in our body and spirit. To do that, we need to renew our minds regularly through God's Word and prayer. The Holy Spirit indwells, teaches, convicts, comforts, empowers, guides, and transforms us. To help with this transformation, Jesus also established the church to renew our minds as we gather for worship. "And he gave some, apostles; and some, prophets; and some, evangelists; and some, pastors and teachers; For the perfecting (maturing) of the saints, for the work of the ministry, for the edifying of the body of Christ" (Ephesians 4:11–12).

Coaches, you can't make disciples unless you're being discipled yourself! Do you spend time on a regular basis reading, meditating, and memorizing scripture? Are you praying regularly for yourself, family, friends, school, church, and your players? Do you attend a Bible-believing church to worship the Lord and grow spiritually? Are you thankful for God's mercies? Do they motivate you to live a life that's sacrificial, holy, and acceptable to Him? Do you *present* yourself daily to the Lord to live and do His will? If you are, God will transform you and help you to be an influence for Christ to your players. It's not our strength but His strength working through us. He wants us to share and embody the Christian values taught in Scripture.

Romans 12 is a gold mine of Christian values God wants us to apply and exemplify! These values are very much a part of our daily spiritual transformation as we grow in Christ. Look at what Romans 12:9–20 teaches us:

- Be loving. "Let love be without hypocrisy." (v. 9, NKJV)

- Be kind. "Be kindly affectioned." (v. 10)

- Be diligent. "Not slothful in business." (v. 11)

- Be joyful. "Rejoicing in hope." (v. 12)

- Be patient. "Patient in tribulation." (v. 12)

- Be prayerful. "Instant in prayer." (v.12)

- Be hospitable. "Given to hospitality." (v. 13)

- Be forgiving. "Bless them which persecute you." (v. 14)

- Be compassionate. "Weep with them that weep." (v. 15)

- Be united. "Be of the same mind." (v. 16)

- Be honest. "Provide things honest." (v. 17)

- Be respectful. "Live peaceably with all men." (v. 18)

- Be disciplined. "Avenge not yourselves." (v. 19)

- Be merciful. "If thine enemy hunger, feed him." (v. 20)

Chapter 6 - PRESENT

As we study Scripture, it's not a coincidence that Paul listed love first in his letter to the church in Rome. In fact, love promotes all the other Christian values he mentioned. When the apostle Paul wrote to the church in Galatia about the fruit of the Spirit, he also began with love (Galatians 5:22–23). When a lawyer asked Jesus which was the greatest commandment in the law, Jesus said, "Thou shalt love the Lord thy God with all thy heart, and with all thy soul, and with all thy mind. This is the first and great commandment. And the second is like unto it, Thou shalt love thy neighbor as thyself" (Matthew 22:37–39). The apostle Paul said, "Though I have all faith, so that I could remove mountains, but have not love, I am nothing" (I Corinthians 13:2, NKJV). The apostle John said, "If we love one another, God dwelleth in us, and his love is perfected in us" (I John 4:12). Everything starts with love!

The coaches I enjoyed playing for the most in high school were the coaches that truly cared about me personally, on and off the court or field. They were good communicators who developed personal relationships. They were concerned about my education, health, family, and friends. I remember one of my high school coaches drove me several hours my senior year to visit a college I had never seen before. Ironically, I ended up choosing that college to attend and graduated from there four years later. If he hadn't sacrificed his time to take me, I may never have known about that school. With God's love working in and through us as Christian coaches, we can establish caring relationships with the players we coach.

Coaches, the most important Christian value you can exemplify to your players is love. "God is love; and he that dwelleth in love dwelleth in God, and God in him" (I John 4:16). Coach John Wooden said, "The coach's most powerful tool is love." Coach Eddie Robinson said, "Coaching is a profession of love. You can't really coach people unless you love them." President Theodore Roosevelt said, "People don't care how much you know until they know how much you care." That's demonstrated through love. "And now abide faith, hope, love, these three; but the greatest of these is love" (I Corinthians 13:13 NKJV).

In Recognition of Our 2006 State Championship Team

Seated left to right: Daniel Nichols, Elijah Gibson, Kyle Bichard, John Mark Conaway, Tyler Jones. Standing left to right: Coach Dan Ellis, Josh Allen, Todd Hughes, Adam Drane, Asst. Coach Dan Morris, Daniel Morris, Judah Longgrear, Ricky Miracle, Asst. Coach Mike Conaway, James Roten (absent).

Chapter 7

PLAYERS

"I thank God, whom I serve from my forefathers with pure conscience, that without ceasing I have remembrance of thee in my prayers night and day; Greatly desiring to see thee, being mindful of thy tears, that I may be filled with joy."
(2 Timothy 1:3-4)

Just like Barnabas mentored Paul, so Paul mentored the young men on his ministry team, such as Timothy, Titus, Tychicus, Onesimus, and others. Paul built relationships and trained these men to be leaders in the ministry. They spent hours together, and after a period Paul would appoint them leadership roles in certain places to minister. As they parted ways, there were no doubt tears as Paul mentions. It's difficult to say goodbye to someone you're close to. Paul often referred to each member of his ministry team as "a son" or "a son in the faith," suggesting these were close relationships.

I remember a time when we were playing in our state tournament at the end of the season. The game was against a team and a coach I respected through many years of competition. Our two teams were evenly matched, and the game went into overtime before we finally pulled out a hard-fought victory. After the game we spoke and shook hands. As we were leaving the court, heading to our respective locker rooms, I glanced over again at the opposing coach and saw his eyes full of tears. I knew from experience what was going on in his mind, and it wasn't the loss—even though I knew that was very disappointing. It was the realization he had coached some of the young men on his team for the last time—guys he had spent countless hours mentoring. It was one of those innocent moments revealing the heart of a coach. It's hard to say goodbye to players you've coached for several years and, in many cases, known much longer.

People have asked me since I retired if I miss coaching and my answer is always the same: "I miss the players." I don't necessarily miss the thrill of victory, and I certainly don't miss the agony of defeat. I miss the players and the relationships I built through coaching. Thankfully, I'm still in touch with some of the players I've coached. It's been a joy to follow their education, careers, marriages, and families, knowing I helped with a small part of their development. I pray they seek and serve the Lord in their lives. I'm thankful for a few who work full time in Christian ministry and others who are faithfully serving the Lord in their local church. I've even had the pleasure of hearing and watching several of them preach.

It's important for us as coaches to remember that our players are individuals God created. He desires for them to be a "new creation" in Christ (2 Corinthians 5:17). I wonder since the apostle Paul referred to some on his team as "my own son in the faith" if he had a part in bringing any to the saving knowledge of Christ? We know Paul at least had a hand in Onesimus hearing the gospel. Onesimus received Christ through faith and became profitable (Philemon 10–11). His life was changed!

Although most of the players I coached at WCCS professed faith in Jesus as their personal Savior, God gave me opportunities to share the gospel with some who were unsure of their salvation. What a privilege that was! Try to sense when your players may need the Lord in their life. Be prepared to share the gospel when you have an opportunity.

The apostle Paul shared the gospel and was a leader that developed leaders. Successful teams need leadership! Over my twenty-two years of coaching, our most successful teams were ones that had strong leaders. "Everything rises and falls on leadership" (John C. Maxwell). Below are ten points on leadership my coaching staff and I shared as we tried to develop leadership among our players.

A leader is one who

- is a good testimony for Christ;
- is encouraging and positive to others;
- works hard at every practice;
- works hard in the classroom;
- demonstrates good sportsmanship;
- is teachable (willing to learn more);
- is faithful (dependable, reliable, trustworthy);
- puts the team first (not self);
- attempts to make their teammates better; and
- keeps others focused on the next game.

Teach and reinforce these ten points to your team. It's also a good idea to sit down with your team captains to review these points on leadership. Remind them why they've been chosen as a team captain and what their responsibilities are to their teammates.

Just as teams need strong leadership, so does our society. We see how important godly leadership is in marriages, families, churches, schools, communities, governments, and businesses. My prayer for the players I've coached is that they'll be godly leaders where God has placed them. Coaches, we can help players cultivate leadership skills they will hopefully carry into their future.

When we look at the apostle Paul in Scripture, we see he was a man of integrity, interaction, influence, and inspiration. It was like a chain reaction! His integrity affected his interaction. His interaction affected his influence. His influence inspired the young men he was leading and coaching. What a great example for coaches to follow in leading and coaching our players.

We need to see beyond the x's and o's. As Christian coaches, our goal should be to have an impact for Christ in the lives of our players.

> "Be an example to the believers
> in word, in conduct, in love,
> in spirit, in faith, in purity."
> 1 Timothy 4:12

Chapter 7 - PLAYERS

In Recognition of Our 2007 State
Championship Team

Seated left to right: Coach Dan Ellis, Judah Longgrear,
Daniel Morris, Josh Allen, Todd Hughes, Jim Wright,
Adam Drane. Back row left to right: Asst. Coach Mike
Conaway, Eric Grubbs, Jadon Smith, Mitch Adams,
Raymond Morris, Justin Gutberlet, Curtis Reynolds,
Manager Davey Grubbs, Asst. Coach Dan Morris.

From left to right: Senior tri-captains Todd Hughes, Judah Longgrear, Josh Allen

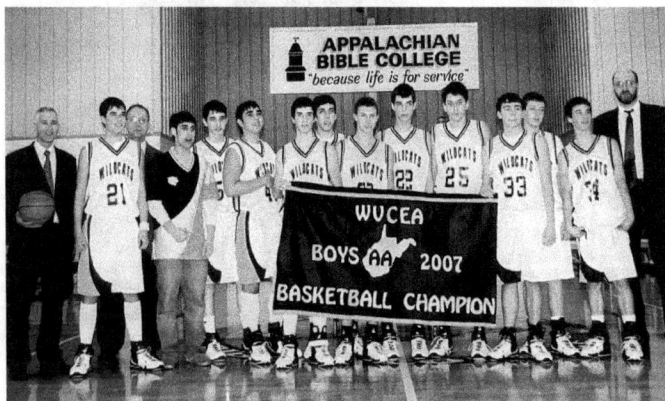

Chapter 8

PARENTS

"Children, obey your parents in the Lord: for this is right. Honour thy father and mother; which is the first commandment with promise; That it may be well with thee, and thou mayest live long on the earth." (Ephesians 6:1–3)

Parents were a big part of our program and our most faithful supporters! The heart of our cheering section at home and away games was parents and extended family. My assistant coaches were all parents who were good Christian role models and had valuable experience and knowledge of the sport. Parents kept our scorebooks, ran the game clock, worked in concessions, led in singing the national anthem before games, helped with transportation, recorded video of games, helped with fundraisers, provided meals, gave devotions, led in prayer before games, and did whatever they could to support our teams.

There's no better example of this than my long-time assistant coach, Dan Morris. Dan coached in our basketball program for over twenty years. He played college basketball at Cedarville University in Cedarville, Ohio, and was very knowledgeable about the game. He and his wife, Donna, had four children—three boys and a girl. All three boys played basketball for WCCS.

Coach Dan Ellis and Asst. Coach Dan Morris

Dan began coaching in our middle school program and then became our junior varsity head coach and varsity assistant. He was a wonderful Christian role model to our players and me. I was blessed through the years to have other parents on our coaching staff with the same Christian character.

I'm thankful for parents, and as coaches, we need to encourage our players to be thankful as well. As mentioned earlier, one of our core values was honor, which means to show respect to others. Players are to "honour all men" (I Peter 2:17), especially their parents! "Honour thy father and thy mother" (Exodus 20:12). When talking to our players about this core value, we brought this to their attention. We wanted them to show respect to their parents. We also had a Parents' Night each season to recognize them publicly for the honor they deserved in raising their children.

As disciples of Christ, coaches should support the parents and each family as best they can. Getting to know parents will help a coach better understand their players. Some players need more mentoring than others because of circumstances in their home. We tried to be sensitive to this, especially when players came from broken homes. Understanding a player's home situation helped me to disciple him better.

Annual Parents' Night recognizing and honoring our players' parents

Depending on a coach's age, they may be like an older sibling, a parent, or even a grandparent figure to their players. Close to the end of my coaching career, one of my senior players that I'd spent a lot of time with over several years told me I was like another grandfather to him! I knew then where I stood, but he meant it as a sincere compliment, and

Chapter 8 - PARENTS

I received it as one because I knew his grandfather. His grandfather was a wonderful Christian man that loved his grandson, spent time with his grandson, and seldom, if ever, missed a game—home or away! His comment to me was an expression of the relationship we had developed. The relationships we build with our players help us understand their needs and come alongside their parents to help meet those needs.

It's obvious from Scripture that the apostle Paul knew Timothy's parents when he began to coach Timothy. He knew they lived in the town of Lystra. He knew Timothy's mother was a Jewish woman and his father was a Greek. No evidence was given that Timothy's father was a believer in Christ. This may be why Paul later addresses Timothy as "my own son in the faith." Paul became a spiritual father to Timothy. Paul knew Timothy's mother's name was Eunice and his grandmother's name was Lois. He acknowledged how their genuine faith in Christ had influenced Timothy. From childhood, Timothy was taught the Holy Scriptures, which made him wise unto salvation through faith in

Jesus. Paul was well acquainted with Timothy's family (Acts 16:1; 2 Timothy 1:5, 2:15).

Coaches, what a great example to follow! Get to know the parents of your players. They'll be a blessing to you and your program, and you'll be better prepared for discipleship in coaching!

Chapter 8 - PARENTS

In Recognition of Our 2010 State Championship Team

Seated left to right: Head Coach Dan Ellis, Nathanael Smith, Curtis Reynolds, Mitch Adams, Raymond Morris, Jadon Smith, Eric Grubbs, Asst. Coach Mike Conaway. Standing left to right: Andrew Gutberlet, Seth Tackett, Cody Gutberlet, Jacob Ungar, Josh Ungar, Kristian Gandor, Asst. Coach Dan Morris.

Chapter 9

PRACTICE

"The things, which you have both learned, and received, and heard, and seen in me, do: and the God of peace shall be with you." (Philippians 4:9)

The apostle Paul was a teacher who demonstrated what he taught. He encouraged the Christians he taught to *practice* what they had learned to grow in their walk with the Lord.

That, in a nutshell, is what coaching is all about! We share knowledge and demonstrate skills so our players can learn the sport. We then have them *practice* those skills so they'll develop into better players and teams.

DISCIPLESHIP IN COACHING

Each summer at Wood County Christian School, we would host a camp called The Total Package Basketball Camp for third- through ninth-grade students. Our purpose was to teach the fundamentals of basketball. When teaching fundamentals, coaches share knowledge and show players proper technique. We would divide our campers into six groups by grade and assign them to one of the six baskets in our gymnasium (two on the main court and two on each side). We assigned a coach to each basket to share knowledge and demonstrate the technique of a certain fundamental. One coach would teach and show the proper way to dribble, another staffer the different types of passes, a third the proper footwork to shoot a right-hand and left-hand layup, another coach the proper stance and movement to play defense, someone else the proper way to box out and rebound a basketball, and another the proper way to shoot a jump shot. Each group would rotate after a certain time to each basket until every group had been with each coach. We would spend half of our camp time each day sharing knowledge and demonstrating fundamentals and the other half having them practice those fundamentals. We would have 3-on-3 and 5-on-5 games to put into practice what the clubbers were trying to learn.

A Total Package Basketball Camp group

I remember an elementary student who began coming to our Total Package Basketball Camp at an early age. He enjoyed basketball and was very coachable. Every year, his ball handling, passing, and shooting skills seemed to improve. As he continued to grow physically and improve his skills each year, he developed a level of confidence that enabled him to excel. By the time he was a freshman in high school, he not only made the varsity team but became a starter, which was rare. During the four years he played at WCCS, he was a member of teams that won three state championships. The key to his success was his desire to practice and master the fundamentals.

Coach Dan Ellis (left) and longtime friend and coach Cam Hayes (right) working together at one of the Total Package Basketball Camps

Understanding and executing the proper fundamentals is so important to the success of individuals and a team. To accomplish this, there must be practice. You've heard the expression,

Chapter 9 - PRACTICE

"Practice makes perfect." Well, no one is perfect, but an athlete can become proficient, and that's the goal for coaches. We want players to learn and develop proper fundamentals to help them become proficient in the sport they're playing.

At the high school level, things aren't much different except the players have grown physically and have a better understanding of the fundamentals. At that point, it's a matter of fine-tuning their fundamentals. Coaches are always trying to improve individual skills and mold those skills together into a team. Every player has strengths and weaknesses, but together they can complement one another as a group. We spent half our practices on improving our fundamentals using a variety of drills. The other half we spent coming together as a team to apply those fundamentals in our offensive and defensive strategies. A practice schedule is pictured on the following page.

Just like sharing and showing is an effective method for coaching, it's also an effective way to disciple our players! Like the apostle Paul, we are to share knowledge and demonstrate that knowledge

Basketball Practice Schedule

Date: 11/10/11
Time: 3:30 - 5:00

Practice No. **5**

Time	Activity	Notes & Comments	Drill Diagram
3:30	Prayer Thought For the Day : Accountability - Definition : Answerable + responsible to a superior or another person - Prov. 27:17 "Iron sharpeneth iron; so a man sharpeneth the countenance of his friend." - What are some ways/areas we can be accountable to each other? (Brainstorm) • Academics / Work hard in the classroom • Practice / Faithful, diligent to practice / prepare • Behavior / Conduct • Spiritually (assign prayer partners)		
3:40	Layups		
3:45	Circle Drill		
3:50	Stretch		
3:55	Stations : (Spend 5 min. in ea. station & rotate on buzzer) Station 1 Rebounding " 2 Dribbling " 3 Shooting (Shoot-A-Way) " 4 Passing		
4:15	Tip Drill Full Court		
4:20	Water Break		
4:25	3 on 2, 2 on 1 Full Court		
4:30	Break up : Varsity & JV (15 minutes)		
4:45	Suicides		
4:50	Free Throws		
5:00	Prayer		

Needed	Emphasis of the Day	Pre-Practice Thoughts	Post-Practice Thoughts	Thought for the Day
Practice Jerseys Balls / Clock Shoot-A-Way Set up	Fundamentals Conditioning	Prayer Christian Value - Accountability	Practice Schedule	Accountability Prov. 27:17

so our players can learn and practice themselves. For example, as we share Christian values, our goal should be to exemplify those Christian values to our players. If we want our players to be respectful, we need to be respectful. If we want them to be diligent, we need to be diligent. If we want them to be faithful, we need to be faithful. If we want them to show good sportsmanship, we need to show good sportsmanship.

We need to lead by example and be Christian role models for our players. That doesn't mean we're perfect because no one is perfect. We all make mistakes because of our sin nature, but our goal should be to strive toward that type of leadership. This comes through a daily personal relationship with our own Coach, the Lord Jesus, and his power working in and through us. "Be strong in the Lord, and in the power of his might" (Ephesians 6:10). He will help us lead by example.

Our practices began with prayer and then, before we started our on-court workout, we would share a thought geared toward helping our players mentally and spiritually. As mentioned, this thought could be a Christian value, one of your core values, a proverb, a verse of Scripture, or another point of emphasis. This "Thought for the Day" complemented our work on the court. It enhanced our goal of becoming the best basketball team we could be for the glory of God. You'll see an example of a "Thought for the Day" in the practice schedule pictured previously.

Use your practice time wisely to have a positive influence on your players mentally, physically, and spiritually. You can accomplish all three! Dave Dravecky, former major league baseball pitcher and author, spoke at one of our Share the Vision banquets at WCCS. He said, "Do not deny the impact your life can have on others."

Dave Dravecky and Coach Dan Ellis

Chapter 9 - PRACTICE

In Recognition of Our 2012 State Championship Team

Front row left to right: Luke Wolfe, Tyler McIntosh, Kalen Gandor, Josh Ungar, Seth Rataiczak, Gabe Strause. Second row standing left to right: Head Coach Dan Ellis, Jamie Arnold, Asst. Coach Dan Morris, Luke Davis, Patrick Goff, Scotty Heslop, Zach Prichard, Asst. Coach Brian Goff, Manager Ben Gray.

Chapter 10

PROMOTION

"Then the king promoted Shadrach, Meshach, and Abednego, in the province of Babylon."
(Daniel 3:30)

The word *promoted* in this verse means "to advance." The words *promoted* and *promotion* can also mean "to increase public awareness." John C. Maxwell said, "Good leadership isn't about advancing yourself. It's about advancing your team." We always felt it was important to advance our players, teams, and Wood County Christian School. And to make the public aware of our current season.

We would begin each season by forwarding a copy of our varsity basketball schedule to the sports editors at our local newspapers. Each newspaper had a daily "Local Schedule" in their sports section, so the public knew where teams were playing that night. We wanted our school to be on their schedule so the public would know when and where the Wood County Christian boys basketball team was playing. Before each season, the newspapers also printed a "Tip-Off Basketball Preview." The insert included a nice article about each area team and game schedules for the upcoming season. We always made sure our schedule was included in the preview.

We also felt it was important to call the results of our games in to our local media so our fans and the public would know how our team did. We had four local newspapers to call our games in to: *The Parkersburg News*, *The Parkersburg Sentinel*, *The Marietta Times*, and *The Marietta AM*. Two were morning newspapers and two were afternoon newspapers. We also had our local TV station—WTAP in Parkersburg, West Virginia— that regularly broadcasted game results in our area.

Chapter 10 - PROMOTION

Everyone keeping up with local news and sports watched WTAP-TV.

We also called our game scores into the Associated Press. So, when their sports sections printed "Prep Basketball Scores," our school's name would appear in every newspaper in our state. This would automatically appear in all our local newspapers as well. It only took about twenty minutes after each game to call our results in, which was worthwhile for our players, teams, and Wood County Christian School. In addition, we kept our schedule and game results updated on MaxPreps, which is an American website that covers high school sports. This well-known website will help promote your team and school.

Over the years of calling in game results, we built a good relationship with the sportswriters at the local newspapers and the sports reporters for WTAP-TV. The newspapers always had a nice recap of our games, which included box scores of our players and our opponent's players. The newspapers would also make it a point to cover some of our home games in person by sending one of their sportswriters. When they did, the game article was usually on the front page of the sports section and included a nice action photo of our players. WTAP-TV also began covering many of our home games, along with other local schools. They would send someone to video portions of our game and then show highlights on their sports newscast that night. We always made sure the final score and the leading scorers were called in prior to the newscast. Our local newspapers and WTAP-TV always did a nice job of covering high school sports in our area.

I remember the first time we took one of our teams to play another school before a Cleveland Cavaliers game at Quicken Loans Arena in Cleveland, Ohio. One of our local sportswriters contacted me to see if he could go with us. The trip was about two and a half hours, and we provided transportation for him to go up and back. His newspaper wanted him to cover our game and the Cavaliers' game to follow. As a result, the next three daily newspapers ran different articles about our trip to Cleveland. One article included a full page of color action photos of our game! The writer included captions for each photo, promoting our players, team, and school. At the time, it would have been difficult for our school to afford a full-page color ad promoting Wood County Christian School, but the Lord provided one for us at no cost!

About a third of the way through each season, our newspapers would start publishing a weekly section called "Mid-Ohio Valley Prep Basketball Statistical Leaders." We always submitted our team stats each week to promote our players, teams, and school. Every season, we had players represented in the different statistical categories in our area.

Because of this promotion effort, our players, teams, and school benefitted. Some of our players were chosen as Players of the Week in different newspapers for their game accomplishments throughout each season. We also had players chosen for Student Athlete of the Week by WTAP-TV, who featured a video interview and game highlights of that player on their morning and evening news sportscasts. Area sports writers sometimes included our players when choosing the All

Mid-Ohio Valley Team and the All Marietta Times Team. Several seniors played in the Battle Against Cystic Fibrosis (BACF) Ohio-West Virginia All-Star Game held each year in Parkersburg, West Virginia, at the end of the season. Other players were featured in articles because of their personal accomplishments and our team's success. A few of our Wildcats went on to play college ball, and our promotion efforts helped in their recruitment process.

Wood County Christian School gymnasium

As a result, public interest in our players, teams, and school also grew. Our home crowds were special! They created a great atmosphere for our teams to play! We not only drew fans from our student body and their families, but local church members became interested as well and attended our games. The gymnasium we built had bleachers on the floor and a balcony with seating on one side above. The balcony wrapped around one end of the court, offering space for people to stand to watch games. On game nights, the environment was electric and exciting. Some matchups were standing room only!

Home cheering section in our gymnasium

Promotion of our players, teams, and school was another incentive for our players to work hard. It always generated excitement. We displayed newspaper articles about our teams in our gym lobby to promote their accomplishments. Students and their parents would see them and be excited to attend our games and support the team.

As mentioned earlier, one of our core values was the word honor, and Scripture teaches we are to give honor to whom honor is due.[3] Promotion was one way we honored our players, teams, and Wood County Christian School. The Lord blessed our efforts and did the rest!

3. Romans 13:7

Chapter 10 - PROMOTION

Promotion of the Most Important News:
The Good News of Christ!

Scripture Regarding Salvation

You need to understand that God wants you to be saved.
"The Lord is . . . <u>not willing</u> that any should perish, but that <u>all should come to</u> <u>repentance</u>." (2 Peter 3:9)

You need to understand that everyone is a sinner.
"For <u>all have sinned,</u> and come short of the glory of God." (Romans 3:23)

You need to understand that sin came from Adam, which resulted in death.
"Wherefore, as <u>by one man sin entered into the world</u>, and <u>death</u> by sin; and so <u>death</u> passed upon all men, for that all have sinned." (Romans 5:12)

"For the <u>wages of sin is death</u>; but the gift of God is eternal life through Jesus Christ our Lord." (Romans 6:23)

You need to understand that God loves you and sent His Son to die for your sins.
"But God commendeth his <u>love</u> toward us, in that, while we were yet sinners, <u>Christ died for</u> <u>us</u>." (Romans 5:8)

"For God so <u>loved</u> the world, that he <u>gave his only begotten Son</u>, that whosoever believeth in him should not perish, but have everlasting life." (John 3:16)

You need to understand that salvation is through <u>faith</u> in Jesus, <u>believing</u> he died, was buried, and arose the third day for <u>your</u> sins.
"That if thou shalt confess with thy mouth the Lord Jesus, and shalt <u>believe</u> in thine heart that God hath raised him from the dead, thou shalt be saved." (Romans 10:9)

You can know you're saved once you believe (trust) Jesus as your own Savior.
"These things have I written unto you . . . that ye may <u>know</u> that ye have eternal life, and that ye may believe on the name of the Son of God." (I John 5:13)

Receive Jesus as your personal Savior today:
Father in Heaven, I believe I'm a sinner and that Jesus died on the cross for my sins, was buried, and arose again the third day. Right now I trust in Jesus and receive Him into my life as my own personal Savior. In Jesus's name I pray, Amen.

DiscipleshipInCoaching.com

PRINTABLE PDF FILES

The following documents are available for you to print out at DiscipleshipInCoaching.com:

Philosophy of Coaching Basketball

Christian Values

The Core Values of WCCS Boys Basketball

Practice Schedules (blank)

Scripture Regarding Salvation

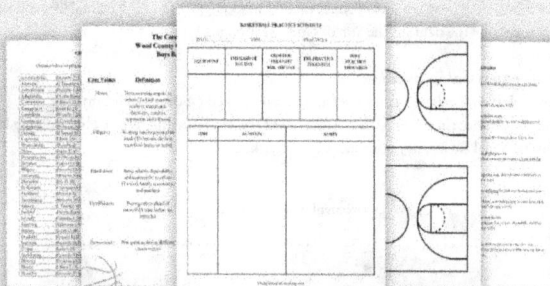

DISCIPLESHIP IN COACHING

RESOURCES

INSTANT PRINTABLE DOWNLOADS - LETTER SIZE